The Signalman

EZRA MILES

THE **BLACK SPRING**
PRESS GROUP

First published in 2023
An Eyewear Publishing book, The Black Spring Press Group
Maida Vale, London W9,
United Kingdom

Cover Art by Daniel McDonagh
Typeset by Edwin Smet

The right of Ezra Miles to be identified as author of
this work has been asserted in accordance with section 77
of the Copyright, Designs and Patents Act 1988

ISBN 978-1-915406-38-5

BLACKSPRINGPRESSGROUP.COM

The Signalman

Ezra Miles was born and raised in Hackney.
His poems have appeared in many publications including
The Cardiff Review, *Tears in the Fence*, and *Ink Sweat and Tears*. He works as
a railway signalman and writes his poems between the trains.
He enjoys playing the banjo and lives in Kent with his wife Emma.
This is his debut collection.

CONTENTS

I climb out from the long wheel base transit van,
all worldly possessions and comforts unloading
to a smoke-strafed, ground-floor flat, snarls cut sharply
across the stained walls, front door off its jamb where
a broken man, the former tenant, kicked it in —
his own house. I smell the hurt, unpack my boxes
and make tea, reflecting on His strange promise.

PASSING SHIPS

Looking out of the window into back garden gloam,
the house-backs have become fused: one long draped

arch, the spine of tiles an ordered shape moving beneath
a coming dark, and the assurance that something continues,

is out there beyond the spindly aerial bones, within the gulf
of plain air hanging, invisible and full. That you could find it

if you only knew where to look, and of course you don't.
We never do. Instead you see the candled clutter of someone

else's life, the nestled warmth, the reddish bloom of home
like a torch through skin. When you see them you disappear,

as if seeing, truly seeing, were an equation, a subtraction of you,
that to look is to be purged of yourself. The view continues

to breathe. And what is it to be seen? When someone looks
at you *you* exist again. The willow tree outside shifts its weight.

Watch the chimney concede a little smoke. Clouds will pass.
Observe the hard white stars begin to talk like colleagues in a bank.

OF THIS WORK; A DISCIPLE

In the yard outside the signal box,
the stocky silhouette in a workman's
jacket removes it, hangs it across
a weathered wooden chair that sits well
on just three legs. He oils a thresher
blade, rubs at the metal as if coaxing
a friction fire. Home's not too far: the house
that juts out like a dislodged tooth, the one
that always smells of damp clothes, old smoke.
He carries on, works at the blade
with an angle grinder: filaments of heat,
tortured jewellery spinning off into
the carbellies and shrapnel scraps.
The light starts to go so he hulks
the salvaged parts back to the must
of the shed. Bad back. A spectral fox
vaults the wall then passes out of sight.
More goes unsaid than can be known.
He forces air out through his lips, turns off
a crackling switch. The horizon bleeds
into a thin red rain. He limps through it
to the van, locks the gate and drives away.
It starts to pour.
The rusted drum of an old machine,
piece by piece, disintegrates.

The box rocks back and forth at the rush of a train,
skeins of new light in the friendship of good weather.
Is it mania, talking to someone who lives
inside of you? But you invited them in. What would
the passengers think? A strange man in dialogue
with (something greater than) himself. What a relief,
that this conversation is neither empty nor dull.

THE LOOM

You listen to the stone and try to hear behind it,
the slow lament of raindrops finishing the trees.
Here the woodland is cathedralled by a canopy of oak
known intimately by the cinders of ancient fire.
It passes from wet moss to ivied light,
it crawls right the way into the stars.
You have become a facsimile of night most dark,
an asteroid rushing to strike a drum.
You howl against the penumbra of life:
this will not always seem to be a great gift given.
Some doorways are sealed for the safety of a child.
See the harsh demon face in plumes of flashing thunder,
the night roils like a blood-broth boiling to paste.
Wear the headdress of loss with willing,
for your loneliness is a privilege, it anoints you,
you will walk against the light until you find
a shadow edging into dark.
In its shade you see a world coalescing malevolently,
but there is a voice crying out from the stones.
This voice longs to sing you back to sanity.
Hear its voice through the wall of trees.
Look past the grey smoulder of dead coals,
it is speaking to you of a true thing.
Every soul has been threaded through the loom of life.
How can you say you are not part of the tapestry?

THE FIRE

After perhaps a minute it wasn't strange
that we were gathered in freezing rain
to watch the firemen, urgent, running

to press half the town's supply against
this graze of heat. A high priest
passer-by, keen to share theology,

says that rain worsens a fire, centring
its glow further into the building's
heart, a blanket warming deeper flames.

That fire is cunning enough to enlist
even freezing water fallen from the sky
is not really a surprise.

I see the fire's living brain from out across
the bay: it breaks the sheath of smoke
to birth itself into the dark, star-fat air,

ruptured orange amid white cream,
cognition dwelling beneath, emerging
like a vein crowning the surface of skin.

The fire sang its threnody to the wood
and steel. '*If the yellow pine catches
it will go like a bastard*'. The old lifeboat house!

The listed hall! Every furnace eventually stops,
and one day the whole world. I would love
to tell you that I stayed all night, brought

cups of cold, still water to scorched men
gasping in their masks and boots,
but no: it was wet. I walked up the hill home,

until the fire became a dim red fingernail
against the bay defying the inevitable,
a mind holding itself to account.

The weather is grim. Rain falls in wavering cords
and the goldfinches are mute under the awnings.
The shack rocks in a strong wind, the sink undulates
as if on a boat. Duties include holding up
traffic, shutting the heavy gates. The signals clear,
droplets are shaken off, the train cuts an open-mouth,
its howl whipping the puddles, shaking the loose slats.

CARVING

The rain drove its music down the chimney,
the television spoke and your breath would slow the room.

Our glow would delicately lower while we sat. Did I notice?
There's no semi-lucid shape beneath a blanket tonight,

it's my ghost-furniture that goes hidden by a white
sheet, no soft groans, no murmurs, no existing between realms.

I mend myself for tomorrow spent at the outpost, my foreign fabric
darned onto this strange land. I hope the threads will blend.

This room has been carved like a great split stone. I do not want
to go to bed alone. Mumbling to God I pray until empty,

the colour of my eyelids waits to brush against a door,
the empty bed begins to churn. In my dream I see you, part-fox,

as you vault the garden wall. It's like you are a forgery
of yourself, the apparition owner of a face not seen in years.

How much easier it would be if you were dead. Time in the box
summons you, you find me in rural outcrops, earning my money.

You find me in my emptiness – on the angular earth I carved
out as my own. How dare you come here as well. I see the traceries

of veins in those shocking blue eyes. A phantom's smile. That distinctive
nose. Where does that magnificent mind rest itself now?

Do you still summon new worlds from your shell pink bed?
Under whose star-slung blanket in which far-flung land do you sleep?

In the silence of work God buoys me softly.
Between trains my face wet with tears, Bible open
on the desk amid poetry and prayer, sweet joy
one could only know from within hermit despair.
The DHL man arrives with a new kettle
and I rush to change myself back, to blot the marked
face of a man nearing the far edge of himself.

AS TWO MEN

'And they have distinct heads, and distinct hands, and distinct souls, and they should be baptised as two men.' [1]

I carry him because I must,
if he faced forward I know
he would carry me so. We
hold no split: like musk mallow
flowers, we stack one upon
the other, foxgloves falling
and melting to one still
greater whole. Not a heavy
load, no, and we walk upon one
set of legs, else I carry him on my back.
We both took the blessings upon our accursed
flesh, and Christ the Saviour made our smote skin anew.
We are seamless. There is no mark where you can tell where Almighty God   the privilege of being
joined us, no thread line. We are together in body though distinct in mind. Swept along.

He carries me, with strength I doubt
I could find, though it takes strength
also to be carried, to never see
ahead, to live in the tailwinds and
wake. We are unified, as one
united in love for the blessing
of life, despite the struggle. I
would sooner gasp the back-
strapped air for a thousand
years than be gone, death
is appalling, despite pain in
this life, I love life and

1 Quote from a Mediaeval German manuscript on the life of conjoined twins. Joined at the back, one twin carried the other.

FEATHER

I went to the woods, alone again, to clear
my heart. I saw the birds alive in feathersoul:
wagtail, magpie, blackbird, thrush, a flurry

of starlings hopping their narrow lives away.
Watched until the clouds thinned, and I faded,
(or at least hoped to), worked hard at it

until my familiar life caught its breath
and jogged out of the treeline towards me.
This is new woodland; slender spruce

and willow. An artificiality about it,
the trees bend thinly to the air like products
on an emptied shelf. The birds insist

that one day here will be real too.
I find in dimly lit green woodlands
that I am not so true. An old argument

recycled, the mind scheming to move house,
or wonders about buying new shoes, or quitting
the job and this fractured, narrow town.

Fragments of the day lodge like petulant
microplastic. The birds, their unimportant
pulses fluttering: I care and I don't, really. I don't.

Maybe silence, like loneliness, is powerful
because it demonstrates what isn't there. It gives
you that rare thing, distance, from the safe projection
of yourself into your everything, everyone.
Would that you might love, no, not yourself, for once,
but love so freely of caveats, conditions,
a whole thing released from us who might constrain it.

FRACTIONS

After René Magritte's *Not to be Reproduced*, 1937

Early day markings
        from the nearest window, luggage
                of history writ large across face.

Light passing over his
        stood gazing at a mirror —
                the absence of lightness,

a surfeit of sculpted
        light in reflection
                reckons, starts the grieving.

Looking back to
        this obtuseness,
                the terracotta man is smoothed,

at that moment knew it all,
        and the next,
                and the next.

WITH FERVENT HEAT

I peered out halfway through the night
to see the blackened larch, and under it
your hot embers rising, drunk before

a captive moon. We locked you out.
Had to. You were too much yourself
for us to bear. But for the beads of dew

that settled upon your pursed lips
you were unanointed, and come midday
you slumbered on, forehead seared like steak

in a smoking pan. When mother let you
in through the back door you stood,
the kitchen glowing red, steam rising

against our domestic air. You swigged
the juice right from the carton fiercely,
and looked at me the same as how a furnace

comprehends a piece of wood. Now, holding
the inert weight of a single bag of ashes
I feel it, realise how light you were.

All that space there had been inside of you
always moving, the liberated air
an inner thing I could not recognise

until now. Nor you. We do it decisively,
you would approve. The bag shaken violently
to get all of you out. We each speak

into the wind before we leave.
On the journey back we pass a bonfire
burning in a neighbour's garden,

daylight nearly gone. A total orange,
absolute, like they were
disposing of the sun.

A man escaped the prison and came up the coast,
breaking into the signal box. He drank greedily
the milk and phoned a friend for a lift, not knowing
the phone records all. They nabbed him in prison greys
a few miles down the road. I think of him, a soul
standing in my little room cloaked in country dark,
smashed glass in the inner sanctum, breath a poison oath.

FOX

Middle of the day and from the window where I'm writing,
I see a fox lying out in the neighbour's garden,

awash in the solace of the sun. His eyes half-closed,
jaw slightly open, the light resting across his thick

orange robes. Today is hot, too. I wonder if he is dead,
and open the window to whistle. An ear twitches slightly

and I realise that no, not dead yet, just taking a rest.
A little while later and a hiss splits the atmosphere.

The fox is up. Dazed, he looks to the house next door.
The grass where he lay retains an echo of his form.

He stands, quietly waiting by the back wall, and watches
as the neighbour throws water at him that doesn't reach.

A lemon half is chucked his way too. He sniffs at it,
that curious long black nose, a slight quiver at its tip.

Then a loud noise and he dashes away, climbing effortlessly
up the garden wall. The shadow of my neighbour

lowers a bicycle from above her head. There's something
so wicked about it all: the refusal to share a moment,

a space, a world with him, one so perfect in his fullness,
his fox-certainty and fox-soul. She swears at his memory

and I close the window, and am alone. In the garden
a police siren peals all around.

The signal box sometimes feels like one of those
initiation tests: go to the wilds, endure
the emptiness of yourself and return reformed.
Confront that which is most you: stray to the dark
realm of your bruised heart and let the light in,
let the grand voice of silence you have always ignored
clear its throat and speak to your newly known smallness.

POEM FROM THE WIKIPEDIA ENTRY FOR 'THE SOUL'

The soul is   the incorporeal essence of a   living being.
Soul or psyche (Ancient Greek: ψυχή *psykhḗ,*
of ψύχειν *psýkhein,*   meaning 'to breathe'),
that the soul must have faculty, its exercise the most   divine
of human actions. Only humans have immortal souls
(though immortality is disputed).
From Old English *sáwol, sáwel,* means immortal
principle   in man, first attested
in the poem *Beowulf,* and in the Vespasian Psalter 77.50.
The Germanic root is thought to mean *'coming from or*
belonging to the sea (or *lake*)',   the belief in souls
emerging from and returning to sacred lakes.
      Old Saxon *séola* (soul)   compared to Old Saxon *séo* (sea).
All living things, from smallest bacterium to the largest
            of mammals *are* the souls themselves (Atman, Jiva),
their physical representative, (the body)   in the world.
The actual self is the soul, body only a mechanism
to the experience   of that life.
Thus if we see a tiger then there is a self-
          conscious identity residing in it,
a physical representative (the whole body of the tiger, observable)
in the world,   such that even non-biological entities,
         rivers and mountains possess.
(*Nephesh*), meaning 'life, vital breath',
         a mortal physical life, but in English
translated as 'self, life, creature, person, appetite, mind, living being,
desire, emotion, passion'   derived from a verb,
'to cool, to blow'   the breath,   as opposed to the body.

Kuttamuwa, an 8th-century Royal official from Sam'al,
requested his mourners commemorate his life
        and his *after*   with feasts,
    'for my soul that is in this stele'

is a sign of God,   a heavenly gem the most learned
   hath failed to grasp.   A soul can be mortal,
         or immortal:
      resides amidst the dreams,
               they have no
                  existence, prior to the
            (eternal)
               life.

'The voice said Cry. And he said, What shall I cry?
All flesh is grass.' Gardens are blooming, yes, verdant!
Like a child holding a captured frog outstretched
to you beside a pond, a soul held by the vast
supernatural that beckons, flesh forgotten,
to participate, here is the invitation.
You are welcomed, clothed anew in a life most obscure.

VISIONS OF A BURNING HOUSE

They plunge straight through a burning basement door,
emerge holding a wriggling log, the high, keening *canzone*

of an ambulance, not like music but the opposite of it.
The couple shake and leap along the road, but not dancing –

and the small red body, not yet really even a body –
this frail universe of one in *crescendo*, is lain

on the pavement outside the charring house,
an oversized rubber mask to its face, the man stopped,

his whole world a *glissando*, and for an instant transfixed
like the rest of us, how unreal it is as the chimney

goes falling through the roof. He is making a sound
like the fire, a noise so much deeper than speech.

She gropes at the baby, its arms like fired clay,
like a living sculpture of itself, like a treble clef

howling out its own *agitato*. The ambulance
doors close and that strange song begins again.

We give the firemen space. They douse it all in grey slurry,
coating the house in a chorus of hoses and lights.

They remain in the road into the darkening night.
Every steaming brick hissing, and a final flame remains,

it glows *cantabile*, then that fire too, no longer singing.

FLESH AND WATER

You, pink heeled and silken
swimming in the silty darkness,

movements drunk by the tide,
the sky beside itself with speckles,

the wind kisses you, disregards you,
blows an inch then a mile.

A fledgling fire on the beach,
you see it start smaller than a pebble.

When the cold comes swimming in
you pull close as you tremble.

DIAGRAMS OF THE HEART

Oh the skin *skin* but what of the maze of love
the high-pillar hedgerows mansions of love
heart in morse code atonal tune chirps
through a deep-sea cable laid across bedrock
oh what about the drawings irresistible
skin crumpled dress sweltering summer
nights curtain discreetly drawn a heavy
velvet weight of love oh tender fibre of lust
what of the salt the flesh the death-wrapping
cloth the bones of lost faces now ghosts
the nevermores blood the groans astonishing
pain of love lost drowned bedraggled souls
died in lust the withered hands that held the maps
hands that held the hand that held the map ache
and rip of love abundant give its brutal take
permanent wounds the marks of love now
mostly lost one often dreamt left to grow
old and shed its gold faked or cruel
oh but could you ever forget the skin?

A monk-for-hire, the hermit monitors his
desolate patch of tallow-stained earth and a vaulting,
gulping sky – in a way like being sick, you find
the spaciousness of self locked inside a box,
as if death falls and you end up somewhere beyond it,
the frequent, plosive voice of a bell, the shock sound
in purgatory, time to render all your duties.

'...AND I MON WAXË WOD'[2]

...and I must go mad

Screaming woman in the supermarket,
distressed and jabbering, weeping-howling,
trapped totally in her own unique cell of pain
as we all stand around watching, unable to help
and scared of her, the swollen pink gnashing
face tear-struck and wet, repulsed too, if honest,
for it is such a scene and we cannot help her,
not me nor the cashier trying or even the kindly
older woman who stops, mid-browsing,
to come over, whispers soothingly to her,
that in fact nothing can be undone, we cannot
save her nor understand what it is engulfing her,
this new language of hurt she lives in,
like an infant and yet somehow terribly adult,
a wisdom twisted up to the surface and left showing
for half a second what life is, how sharp it can be,
before it sinks back again, so we stand and watch, fearing
she may never be empty, that she has riven one
colossal seam through herself which cannot
mend, and we are there, reminded that it
shall one day arrive.

2 The title is taken from 'Fowles in the Frith', an anonymous Medieval lyric poem.

One day I had a panic attack, alone whilst
working in the nowhere void of potato fields
and duplicated barns, hollowed out markless roads.
Every breath was a treasure. Somehow, each one came
after the last. The trains went by. It passed. Grey walls.
I was ashamed to call for help, admit the cracks.
Back to the empty flat, I drank the silent win.

PUSHING AT AN OPEN DOOR

Or could he be a wanderer? If not stuck
inside this honeycomb of breath-stilled air,

could be a seeker if he wasn't always pinned,
a specimen-in-waiting beneath the halogen, severe,

the body paused in passing beyond. Isn't that
just the way? That the body snuffles for comfort,

warmth: his limbs repeating their factory work
in ant rhythms, the assembly of matter into form.

The same stripped light there too, he works beneath
a halo fastened overhead. You hope he would accept

the night, so keen to press against his sparrow
shoulders, that one day he will leave, walk out through

the fire escape, and go for many miles far beyond
the industrial estate, until he finds the signal fire

up on high, suggesting a path. Perhaps he would
see before that glistening meadow a leaping hare

– its body threadless, trembling! Or else hear
a humble name outspoken, waiting for his claim.

HUNGRY GHOST

Sky
outside
near
black,
a
dog
sighing
on
blankets
sat
beside
freezing
perishing
youth.

The
little
boy
between
worlds
looks
out
from
his
window,
traces
marks
of
scars

yet
unmade
across
landscape
outside,
then
traces
again
across
his
own
reflecting
rain
face.

TREE LINE-BREAKS

I watch the movement — cold sun on late water,
the day marks its exodus in ripe orange.
I sat for a thousand hours by the cool damp
eyes of the pond, listened to the heartbeat of God,
saw the hurly-burly of two drakes passaged
as light through the reeds. Or else I said so.
What is truth? Before it's noticed it's written
and stowed in a sack. At home, plucked
and carved. I dress it and serve.
A man needs to eat.

Meister Eckhart, the Christian mystic, once shared
'There is nothing so resembles God like silence'.
You coach the ear to catch those great voids of Himself,
the emptied peace that gathers everywhere between
all other sounds. The sound of nothing, that cool pond
amid the chirping blessings of the goldfinch flock
that fill my soul entire on their morning visit.

ENDLING[3]

I'm sick to death of dreams.
        The last old man left in my mind
    floats raindrops hooked on strands
            of radiance, his weak eyes blinking in lights
                leading onwards to
        the always roaring pool. Sits
      threading his question, knuckling
silver gills and floating. He works
                his hands. Lonely little mask
      of a man unflagging, a lap
full of gasping fish who
        blink and couldn't care less, lucent
            petals on their meat absurd.

      Their light slowing now.
        Maybe because of the dark coming, maybe.

Holding on is its own reward.
      A cask full of fish with bright eyes.
            Storm coming later and he blinks,
    marking time,
        but the sky is sick with dreaming,

    so stop it.

3 A word originating in the scientific journal *Nature*, to describe the last known individual of a species.

On rare days off I walk into the shell-shocked
town centre: a statue of a forgotten saint opens
his arms to bless the market from beneath
a glaze of pigeon-shit; the empty, shuttered shops
moan. But the dense, silt-brown river is teaming
with bright silver fish, the young men cast from the banks,
you recall, He made them fishers of men, those boys.

KEEPER

Observe the alien white form
        in a forensic cotton suit,
                the opaque veil, crowned

by striped atoms in swirl.
        How is it that the air
            we breathe is the same

as theirs? What words would fill
        their narrow throats, if they
            had need for words at all?

Their legs, their lungs
        caked with quivering pollen,
            their gasps unheard even

by each other. The sun's
        eternal shape persists as if
            brand new. I see the soul,

man alive, I see it all,
        and lay no claim upon
            those busy lives manoeuvring

through this skim of sky.
        A hand terraforms both
            our worlds, coats it

afresh in quixotic smoke.
        My own breath passes
            through the gauze, mingling

with theirs and yours.
        Their wings reverberate
            like a tuning fork.

Maybe I needed it: the harsh, smarting slap
of this dependence on God. No frills, nothing slick,
only the run-down old box and a simple, rugged
wooden cross. Just the bending knee, found yielding
to holy love, the lonely cry to be held and known,
to be stripped of self-decided graces then returned
them, only now I see whom it was that gave.

RUACH[2]

I

A black sun rose on the shattered tiles of failing roof,
half the kingdom contained and sterilised.

It phases the kebab shop in charnel light. The meat
will drip, fat cascading down a red grate glow.

In my mouth the sorrow of our lives placed on hold,
furniture under plastic sheets, mandatory meditation

routines in bedrooms o'er the land. Someone in a care
home beneath faded walls, under more plastic sheets.

Everyone is relearning how to breathe, how to pray.
People nestle outside the window like doves.

They eat burnt offerings from styrofoam shells.
They gulp chilli sauce in their cars as if they will be saved.

They lower then replace the mask between mouthfuls.
You wonder if their lips could speak this as a psalm.

I feed a starving fox smoked salmon on our steps.
It looks back, mistrustful eyes and quick wet teeth.

2 'Ruach', the Hebrew word for spirit and breath. It is also translated to mean wind.

II

Tell me
the one about
the mushrooms
that grew in a shed
amongst enforced night,
foreverdark in rarefied air,
and now comes that puncture
of breath, gasping to bring the
true light to the spores, tell me it
again, you who understand so well
the weight of a word against a world.

III

The sun slides behind
a block of flats. Imagine
a tombed monk's fingertips,
his blackened creature-paw
a brittle bunch of pods.
Where a light once dwelt
it will dwell again.
A sealed eye will open.
This prayer began
before you awoke
to claim the air
as breath.

IV

Someone set one of the barrels outside
The White Hart alight. I saw it, incarnadine

between the chained benches of a locked-down
pub, a distaste of scorched hops on the air.

People cloister inside the kebab shop, the men
charred by a blush of coal. Our calcified breath

leaves the residue of a prayer in the walls.
That same vision comes back when I'm in bed:

of a burning barrel, like that village down south
where they carry them upon their backs, fire drip

and scalding tar, but this one eerie, alien and alone,
burning like a harsh cough, like a funeral pyre.

GOURD

Your husk is dry and smooth as paper, the outer edge
a burnished leather spread thin, as if it remained

fragile in its own eternity of frailty, as if its turgid
past did not precede it, as if I couldn't hold it

and feel immediately the absence of presence,
the lightening of a life which you now know so well.

Your hospital bed dwarfed you, the strange hinge
in its centre operated by a secret finger,

a mechanism that suspensefully raised your gaunt
and howling gourd up to level with my eyes.

You turned that poor and withered ape-like head away
and I swear I saw the blood move through the tropic blue

vein that tunnelled your temple, your downy ears,
the tufts of brittle white grass, the rheumy eyes elipsed

in pink, the mouth aquiver, stuffed with some
phantom bolus I later realised was your swollen tongue.

And yet, how odd, there was also an unfamiliar iron
to your grip, some vitality of force when you held

my hand in yours – not the other way around. All this
emptying out had made so much space for a new spirit

to fill you – like new wine in an old skin, and I saw
your wine and could name it, and together

in that moment we both did hold, and weep, and drink.

I get ill from Covid and shiver two long weeks,
lying in bed embalmed in wool like a relic
emptied from a chilly tomb. Fever comes each night.
I hallucinate the voice of many chanting saints,
swirling around the room their prayers, a voice proclaims
Him 'Holy, Holy, Holy', the sweat soaks straight through
into the sheets, the shape silhouetted an angel.

A NEW CHURCH

After Pieter Bruegel's *The Harvesters*

The women replace their
tall white hats and bob
into the burning gold.

I squeeze a holy clod
of earth, I intend not
only to take but serve.

Line meets stanza at the taut, clean miles of rail-track,
it carries us over empty fields unlettered.
A lonesome shape slumping enormously across
earth; the anonymous passenger; all noticed
and watched by His patient, present eye. He writes
the best verses in us. Have you not noticed how
life bends willingly to something so like a poem?

CEREBELLUM

I name the poem cerebellum, after the
strata of the brain controlling motion.

See the scattered run of a muntjac,
its silhouette a charcoal drawing

bounding up the sheer wall of the valley.
He was scratched at half darkness

against the ridge, as though a
glyph had taken to running.

It was his extant shadow, floating
up against the hillside, perhaps

the finest of all the poems I've read.

PRAYER

I sense the shift of power always
on entering the nether-shade,

a sharp and piping wind beneath
coverings of branch and leaf,

twisted wood and blooded thorn.
I bend my knee as though a fawn,

and there it is, it feels like weeping.
I empty out the words and seeds,

I break a twig and rend my clothes,
a bead is dripping from my nose.

Here now I see spectres of pain
pass through and up, to canopy.

For it is your sacrifice actually,
amid a small voice held in the rain,

your offering, your totality,
your tender blood clings to my hair.

Your spilt sap holds me tight as glue,
the copse is silent but a presence there,

another hint, another hidden clue.

Morris is burning something in the back paddock:
the sliding mountain of smoke travels all the way
onto the tracks. The trains are invisible, cloaked
until the last moment; the uncorked metal like
a glass face pushing forward like the masthead
on an old ship, something you would carve to disturb,
a wretch-face in grimace, born of dark, oily fire.

TRANSFORMATION POEM

I became a sword that was being held in someone's hand,
then became the laughter that was heard upon the mountain,
then I was rain, and probably fire, though this was so long ago
it's getting hard to remember. Then I was a frog, pond-diving,
sliding between dimensions, then I became my father, his silver
beard removed from behind the ears (it was on a wire).
After that I became a neglected dachshund, my belly scraping
in the shelter. At some point during this time I was the sound
of one hand clapping, and then I was the hand itself!
Then I became the colour of royalty, a rich purple banner,
gently flowing, and then I was not just its colour but one
myself, a gilded king in shimmering raiment dangling
a gigantic set of keys, and after that I expected I would become
a pauper, though it didn't, funnily enough, happen. No, instead
I became a yardstick, used to measure length, a simple tool
which determines values unemotionally. I should probably
also mention that I was an island, and a vessel, and a pudding,
a cargo crate, plus a speedboat and an orange. I lastly settled as
an egret, my long, bandy legs striding through a stagnant river
of meanings, my keratin-face long, with harsh narrow eyes
facing forward. In some way above it, two slow beats of those wings
and I was gone, floating loosely against the soft, marshy sky.

I WAS WALLS

We marked the flag at the highest point
with a painted albatross – our cargo drove the birds away.

This bounty was heaved to shore, half a payload
short, turned yellow and tossed overboard.

The wooden ship would speak, I remember
her wet skin gulped the quivering air,

the crucible at her centre a furnace, a black cage,
men would swoon and choke down in her core.

The world back home was jammed with noise,
and arriving I was afraid to speak, my voice half torn.

My back now sculpted by flings of the whip, my hands
did ring, in the port I drank until an eye would bleed.

Each afternoon I'd awake, still cut, from dreams
of peony fields and soft pink silks. I would struggle

out onto a low, stout boat. To the nearest shoal, our nets
dangled like a broken wrist, my mouth a knotted rope.

We'd pull them in and heave; white thrashing air, their
bodies glisten, shiver back, alive.

And looking now to the cold fish-eyes of each catch,
in the wet iron trapped against the weave,

their gasped throats latched and snared,
I see you, and them, and me.

PROCESSION

They travel, holding furnaces in themselves,
footsteps melding into the blue night's weight.
Behind trail hungry dogs, wild children
and their mothers wear darkness as a medal.
In loose formation, men with collars starched,
teeth glowing through cold corridors of moon.
Tight fingers clamped safe as houses around
old-fashioned cases. One of them is selected,
he swallows all their secrets as if a sinful bread,
and now they traipse together a procession,
moving through night, riding on the air like salt,
disappearing into candles, car parks, vaults.
Some will find their ways to the cobbled
courtyard of the old villages, to take their
bedding place for the night inside a fountain,
drained. Others sink back into the scaffold
of the city, dual-carriageway like smoke
in urns, they drift up, the exodus an aeon.
The road reappears like good cards, shadow
bones fanning into the night, their faces marked
lush topaz, atop the scars we start with.

A cat was struck by a car on the crossing.
The owner was told. She didn't take his body,
hard as a board since last night spent frozen outside
and splayed by the road. I place him, an orange
universe of cat, in a black sack, his animal
truth left beside the bins. A man in a hi-vis
collects to incinerate, ash eddies in the wind.

KINGDOM

The river has called for you. You step onto the light of day,
you climb from a granite tunnel carved into the mantle.

The water has formed small grey pools in your feet
and it soaks you. A pale spider hanging from a hollowed tree,

dangling by its own silken atoms. You wrap your fingers
around it, feel its tension. The spider runs across your hands

as you turn them in the sunlight. Watch it melt into the shine
and appear again in the darkness, thin limbs like hair, you can

barely feel it. *See* it. The river has called for you and you
must answer. Your shoes have worn away. On the shale path

the ground pierces your foot, the sole-blood mingles the earth,
its colour changing. The land slopes into broken clouds

as the jagged air sticks inside your chest, its moisture waiting
on your eyelids. You walk into the guttural river. The water

bathes your bloodied feet, the current callous and enduring.
Cold migrates to bone. Feel the cut of rivers past and think

of every man, woman and child who stood in this water,
felt their heart flood, their teeth chatter. Your breath sharp

as you break the water, the sky now clearing. Look up to a light
rain falling. Your fingers are river beds. Beside you is the mountain.

ELIJAH

The dishevelled sackcloth house, roof pitched
concave like a starving man's pantaloons.

A chipped cup brims with rainwater, the woods
rustle something approaching a prayer.

Carrying drips of hot light through the meld
of wood – I find a nest unhatched, a build

of stray hairs, mucus and spit. I hold them, fragile,
so nearly alive. Someone has to take, and so I did,

my pockets filled with those cooling eggs,
a dark shape at home in the emboldening dark.

I enjoy the drive to work: country roads through flat
muddy fields of newly turned earth, the combine
harvester's outrageous, titanic efficiency
rocking in front of me. The machines belt out growling
songs of service. They hurtle past my box, bored lads
with headphones in driving, they spend this slender life
soil-deep, coaxing, stewing the land to plenty.

TRUE NIGHT

The old lamps found us our route, field dressed in sheer skirts
of pitch. Night hems drag the edge beside a ridge of oaks,

farther out the ancient wood where he with tall-heeled boots
walks, chest lit on fire and mouth full of bats. A wailing

choir of one. Swollen old girl smells like blood and cream.
We sought the changeling and caught it, dragged it from her,

clamp our hands around hoof and yank at that torn wet hole,
red-blue ropes of spirits that shelter inside a birth-fat cow.

The calf is near death: his piebald legs can't find the earth.
She has started to lick him clean, her broad grey tongue

warm and veined. The boy notices first. Atop his head a slit
between soft velvet face, fur still glazed in holy strands.

We push the slit open, reveal between those two glossy
conkers a third, dead eye rolls of its own volition, unseeing.

The smell of rotten fruit. We carry the calf away,
its unmothered body tensing at the jab of cold. True night.

I slit the throat and he bleeds out, blood upon coarse frayed
grass, snarling woods. We recognise omens when we see them.

Somewhere out there, in the tree-scream, he parades, a lurid
shape, twisted faerie limbs in endless dance. I disrobe the calf.

The meat marks a reluctant offering left in a steaming heap.
We make the sign of the cross. I lead the boy's hand.

SOLAR POWER

Could we stay awhile here,
in the apricot memory of dawn?

I'd rather be here. The morning light
persists and the trains will not run.

Your mouth is mending: laces eye to hip
to soul, a mutual skeleton of urge.

Ahh, but duty calls: there's a place
for me to be. I have to go.

We shall live once, yet it seems
already a thousand turns of the cup.

I'd shut down the country for you.
I would siege Nineveh. I'd die in my boots

for one more morning of you, your breath
ghosts its fog like a perishing god.

What if Christ was out there, labouring the fields?
Or in the room too, pulling levers, talking shop,
sharing a sandwich and filling up the teapot,
passing comment on the train stock, the rail head
condition, generally making Himself useful?
When all this is condemned, the box pulled down to dust,
will He ask 'How are you, friend? How's work been going?'

THE SCAFFOLDER

for D.A. McDonagh

His footsteps packed
        into the long-bed truck, name
                wiped from the foundation stone,

a hump of rails against
        his shoulder, he builds what could
                be an ark. I heard him ask

when bent to earnest knee
        for help to draw, 'Lord, guide
                my hand, let it be your sketch.

I do not want to steer
        the coal, do not want to lug the pole
                over a red clay worksite floor'.

He waits, a kneeling child
        among clanging noise to spot
                the dove of truth breach the sky,

the wych elm to betray her
        mystery, for rain falling on tarpaulin,
                for the scaffold to come down.

14 LINES

Death would be a mercy. You don't deserve it.
I sentence you to live forever, no line break
just one long stanza, an endless present spent
inside the rhyming couplet, another life that
starts and refuses to end, the days only greyer,
the rain only harder. I look to God and my
sordid, defiant demon hates him. My one
worthwhile fragment of soul, His domain, feels
farther, starker. I am angry at my poverty,
I take it out on the poem: little music in this
verse. A life refined under quatrains of rage,
lust and diminished fire. I cannot redraft, won't
edit. I would give more if I had it. Or I would
take it again and write it, and so have it.

Jesus Christ, Holy One of Israel, how could you sit
beside me on the foam-depleted chair? But you did.
In fraying hope I heard your breath, shared your prayers
through scything black night. I wait here for the phone
to ring, to send me home. I know He is here with me
in the insanity of that which was emptied out.
That the Living God, a friend, would not let me alone.

CREPUSCULAR

Talking to Emma about the word,
we agree it sounds wrong, as though
it were destined for another, more robust thing.

'It sounds like something of matter –
maybe a thing quite angular'
she says, and I see a territory of bones,

a muscle twitching, a jutting jaw.
What it means, actually, sits softly:
the split measure of twilight,

of the place that arrives when
the moment tears itself, is held
in half-luminance, as if light and dark

were two voices having that same
conversation every evening, one
helping the other to paint the trees blue.

CATCHING

Slow light broiling. The dark lip of a window. A buttery moth
has come in,
                        crossed the threshold and now here she is.
She must be feathermade,
                        to flick and surf the soup of air
beneath those curtain wings,
                        the moth small and smooth as
drops of cream.
                        Fractures in the folds of her knees.
A line of stark shadow
                        spreads along the fireplace.
I am a fracture too, then.
                        A hairline crack
runs right the way through me.
                        They always fly back in, the window
open mouthed, the sun
                        disappearing like a sinking spoon.
Other moths I would kill,
                        my palms two moist and smashing walls,
moths pestled into a golden paste,
                        a dust pulverised from
their shining flakes.
                        This one comes back in,
                        caught this time from below
    in a gentle cup
                        and she leaves lopsided,
meandering towards the gathering black,
        a new gold
                        with all its permissions
    minted to her wings,
while the men in their houses
                        with their hands firm as hammers
open windows, and turn on their lights.

One of the goldfinches that I like watching frisk
the air swoops as if poured straight from God's majestic
pen and, flitting through the wideness He allows, flew
in through the open window. It stopped two inches
across the threshold, hung in the void I sit in
every day, hovering an instant then leaving
white sky. In an absent bird I understand God's grief.

KEN, DANCING

For Ken Sequin

Each time the video loops he disappears,
his ghost-fragment gone, the Greek music
at crescendo begins again, Ken, dancing
for Iliassa, who is not there. He shuffles,
adrift in frame, pirouettes and churns,
moving his Crocs against the cold air,
the bare floor, the soft bulb, the ascending
limb that shimmies its delight, even
alone we must dance, for the private music
that we rarely hear tonight demands it.
Old thumbs remember the weight
of a favourite hand, the density unique,
their memorable mass and soul-weight.
The creep of watching a moment that wasn't
yours, of stealing someone else's subtle form.
Ken is dancing inside a video and then he's not.
The soul is only weighed by being gone.

AVOCET

After work I drive to the marsh. Too much
time inside the box and no friends, no voices

to overhear, just the rarified thoughts of solitude,
the low and tragic station life inevitably yields to.

I see it strafing across the upper bank, tinted
underneath by the floodplain's grey shine.

Angled like a bend in a branch it glides as if
depression, the dark-faced avocet of your own life,

had no licence to sheer the corridors of thought,
no permit to drive on the winds. A bird against all-air,

arabesque in coasting turn, this stranger journeys
through light's gables, ladders an invisible seam of sky

with long stiletto bill furrowing. And so I remember how
birds are encased in their own language of sorrow,

and I cannot bear the prospect of a world without
beauty, nor to lose one single avocet from my eye.

In the harsh timbre of its song, unthinking and
strangled, I know I mustn't leave this hallowed earth,

no, not until night arrives of its own volition,
to pierce life's strange and swooping tune.

From the solitude of an almost-grave you hear
the rushing, frantic prayers mewled out inside the stark
box, a hutch for your soul — like a bulb on at night
forever. No savour, no dreams to stir horses
cantering in your bones. You are here all the time,
the cup of tea smouldering gently, it leaves a
Saturnalian ring carved in the waxed wood floor.

VIEW FROM THE FAIRWAY

Coming through the gate into the hollow of another
solitary afternoon, I tread from the dappled path
of the manicured golf course, and passing in
between the hooded pines, walk into the grove.
I give nothing to this place, for I have so little to offer,
so instead I take. My eyes take on slow, greened light,
the somnolent stillness a union of trees in canopy make.
A frond of spruce rubs its waxen charm into my skin,
I place it against my skull – that grim, grey
territory which always eats but is never filled.
I take the coo and purr of the woodpigeons mating
above me, the mournful striation of a restless blackbird,
deep into my ears. I hope for a nest to be builded
here, some caved abode for a glowing egg.
Lastly, and perhaps the only thing I cannot keep: a sureness
of the sureness by which His hand shields.
Linger in the musk of life in spite of life itself – goodness,
you have to grasp it, this strange gift, and take it as your own.

I am duty bound. I think of the centurion
at Vesuvius. I am here I will not turn.
I nearly put my back out pulling the levers.
A thick chain yanks the arm of a raising signal.
I wear my failures as a monk would his sin,
upon my body, close as a glove. I atone.
There are duties for me to perform out here, I know.

CONVERSATION OVERHEARD AT THE HATCHING OF AN EGG

'Let me tell you something about the birds:
God chose to let them merge into the ecstasy of air

but not understand what flying means when we say
flying, when we imagine it with our eyes closed

like you're doing now. They don't even know they're
doing it! They have songs too, but don't know *what*

singing is, what it's for. It's the price they pay, and it's fair,
no? Ok, so what do we get? We get to know. We get

let in on the secret as we stand around, looking up
at them. Sometimes it feels more like a curse.

Every bird that sounds its voice or meets the sky
will answer to God. He speaks to each of them,

whispered everything long ago, spoke it
straight into their wings. It lasts forever,

far beyond the fire they consumed, it holds on inside
the ash, the breeze. He feeds them all, even those that die.

Call me crazy, I don't mind. But listen for a moment,
please. Please? Soon all this will end.'

An astonishment of light baffles the box.
Christ is Risen! He is here yes I see Him,
the sun released from behind Morris' yard
to wring a golden-pink weariness from all.
The march flies are swirling outside, the cornfly
come in the warmth to speckle my arms with
their life, the bells are ringing, are ringing.

ACKNOWLEDGEMENTS

I would like to thank *Queen Mob's Teahouse* for initially publishing 'And I mon waxë wod', *Ink Sweat and Tears* for publishing 'Kingdom' (then titled 'Empire'), the *Utopia Project Zine* for publishing 'Of this Work; a Disciple', *Riggwelter Press* for publishing an earlier version of 'Catching' (then titled 'Moth') and *The Cardiff Review* for publishing 'Transformation Poem' and 'Elijah'. An earlier draft of 'Fractions' (then titled 'On Variable Foot') was published in *Foxtrot Uniform*, and 'Endling' was published in *The Gronthee*. Thank you all for giving my poems a place to live.

Two poems, 'True Night' and 'As Two Men', were written during my residency at the Wellcome Collection. I am indebted to them for their support and encouragement, in particular to Dr. Elma Brenner for her maverick approach to research and collaboration.

I am very grateful to all the friends who helped read my work, most notably Neil Hunter and Angharad Overton. They are all wonderful writers, poets, artists and musicians, and their help and support was essential for the development and refinement of these poems.

My great thanks to Daniel McDonagh, not only for his critical ear to my poems, but also for his wonderful drawing of the signal box on the book's cover.

This list would also be incomplete without mentioning my wife Emma, whose love, encouragement, advice and patience amaze and sustain me. Thank you.

I am so grateful for my editor, Catherine Myddleton-Evans. Her careful and generous readings of many drafts of my poems plumbed the depths of these poems and developed them into a unified collection. Many thanks also to the Black Spring Press Group, especially to Amira Ghanim, who aided me along every step of organisation from submission to publishing.

Lastly, an enormous thank you to Dr Todd Swift, who supported me throughout writing and development, shaping the direction of these poems and their focus. This collection would not exist without you. Thank you.

All glory to God.

Ezra Miles